THE REALISTIC TRADER

Other Resources by

Siam Kidd

'Hedging Against Uncertainty' DVD. A Complete Guide to Safely Investing in Gold & Silver

www.HedgingAgainstUncertainty.com

'The Investors' Insight'. Keeping an eye on the Markets, so you don't have to.

www.SiamKidd.org/investors-insight

'The Crash of 2016' DVD

www.TheRealisticTrader.com

D0493907

Siam Kidd

Siam is an ex RAF Pilot turned full time Currency & Commodity Trader/ Gold & Silver Investing Specialist. Editor of the *'Investors Insight'* monthly publication and producer of the DVD 'How to Profit From the Crash of 2016.

Siam joined the RAF after school and not long after completing his Officers' Training he began trading & investing. He didn't have the most successful of starts. Being completely self-taught and impatient he quickly lost a fair amount of money and savings. This continued for some time as he continually struggled to balance his pilot training and trading. Eventually trading became quite profitable for him.

In his mid-20s, Siam began to excel at trading and investing and it wasn't long before he was making some sizeable profits and also a number of successful key economic forecasts despite contrary mainstream opinion. He openly admits that he never wanted to teach currency and commodity trading as 'FOREX trainers' tend to all be tarnished with the same brush, however due to strong demand, The Realistic Trader was formed. Founded on the principal that these trading workshops be completely transparent, rich with content and putting the students in front of profits. These courses have been attended by people from all walks of life and the feedback has been beyond all expectations.

Alongside this, he has accurately forecasted many major economic events like the 2012 Apple stock crash, 2 Bitcoin crashes (accurate to 2 weeks) and several Gold and Silver moves. His chilling evidence of another Stock Market Crash within the next 18 months is now gaining traction around the industry. He lives in Norwich with his wife and family and despite being extremely risk-averse with trading, is a keen adrenaline junkie.

His favourite hobbies are Aerobatics flying, Helicopter flying, Sky-Diving and Skeleton Bobsleigh in which he was on the RAF team.

CONTENTS

THE DON'Ts

What This Is Not...

"I could probably write a book on the topic of frustration and anguish from losing large sums of money..."

Congratulations and welcome! This book is simply the product of years of heartache, dwindling bank accounts, clenched fists and a whole lot of other pains and frustrations. You see when I first started out trading, I really had no idea of what I was doing. I knew absolutely nothing about economics and whenever the subject of finances and investing came up in conversation I would glaze over in a mini-fear hoping that no one would ask me a question or my opinion on interest rates or derivatives etc. These conversations may as well been in Swahili for all I knew. However I've always been really good at anything I set my mind to, and combined with my hunger for more money and expensive doodads (like most teenagers do), I figured I'd be able to pick this trading malarkey up rather quickly. I mean, if I can fly planes in the military, how hard can financial trading be?!

As you can guess, this *'Yeehah'* attitude subsequently lost me over £50 000 in my 1st year of trading. Trading really is an odd topic. Everyone has an opinion on it, yet most are ill-founded. And only now that I'm out of the murky clouds can I categorically say that **trading the markets is the single most frustrating yet rewarding life-skills that one could learn. And it's actually one of the easiest.** It really is. I really cannot put into words the liberating feeling of knowing you can grow any amount of money between 3-15% per month. I now know that I will always be able to put food on the plate for my family just from trading. And the way I trade really does boil down to 'buy this when these indicators do this, sell this when these indicators do that'. I'm not joking when I say a 12 year old can do this...I'd know because I've already successfully taught a 12 year old to trade... next...my wife...

Now before that previous paragraph gets completely misunderstood, let me clarify a few points:

i.) Trading is very easy. It really is. As long as you have the right training, information, education and the correct strategies, it really is a doddle. However, if you don't have all of those components, trading will be the easiest thing to eat up all of your hard earned cash, chew you up and throw you out onto the pile of traders who consistently lose money on the markets. (*That's 96% of all traders by the way*). I really do have to stress this point, if you're not properly prepared, you will lose more money, a lot faster than you could ever do in a casino! You wouldn't put your 17 year son/daughter into an F1 car would you? So if you are doing what I first did, (Googled a bit, opened up a live trading account, then blew that account in a day...then continued to repeat this cycle), then please **please** stop what you are doing and go back to the drawing board. This book is a great place to start.

ii.) Trading is a **life-skill**. It shouldn't be treated as anything else but this. It is not a way to 'Get Rich Quick', but it's a **life-skill** which will enable anyone to semi-retire within 10 years. Or even 5 years if you're dedicated. So remember, if you treat this as a 'Get Rich Quick' scheme, it will 100% result in a 'Get Poorer Quicker' scheme. Trust me on this...I've been there. A few times now...

So, sit back, get comfy and read on. I really hope you find it an informative read and forgive me if I'm rather blunt on a few points, but I really do have to emphasize a few things now and again. Despite being a successful full time trader now, I've learned the hard way by having 8 years' worth of mistakes under my belt and I've made every mistake one could possible make...at least twice. So if you take all of this in and heed these pointers, I **guarantee** you that this tiny book will save you tens of thousands of Pounds...

Best wishes,

Siam

P.S. *The following Chapters are in no particular order or significance...*

<u>WHERE IT ALL WENT WRONG...</u>

Back in 2005/06 when I was fresh out of school and in the middle of my RAF Officers' Training at RAF Cranwell, I was extremely naïve. In pretty much every respect. I wouldn't have admitted this back then, but up until that point I had led a rather sheltered life compared to my other Officer Trainees. I wasn't from a wealthy family but my parents worked like slaves in order to send me to one of the best private boarding schools in Norfolk – *Gresham's*. I really respect and thank my parents for the long sacrifices they had to make to send me there.

As school-boarding hours were from Sunday night to late Saturday afternoon, I definitely had no 'street-wisdom'. I didn't do Economics at school and so up until the age of 18 I had literally zero knowledge of business, investing, money, politics or any of those 'grown-up' topics. Ignorance really was bliss, until I remember one day I was chatting with a bunch of instructors and my Commanding Officer and conversation turned to the Stock Market. They may as well been speaking in Swahili for all I knew and I suddenly felt really uncomfortable. I remember getting all nervous and just dreading the inevitable questions of, *"What do you think Siam?"* or *"Where do you see the FTSE going?"* First of all, I didn't have a clue about the Stock Market and what the hell was the '*Footsie*'?

Thankfully, the questions were never fired my way...mainly because I quickly sneaked off to pretend checking that my Bergen was all squared away. It was from that moment onwards that I quietly promised myself to never be clueless in that department again. All of a sudden I had this newfound urge to become at least credible when talking about these scary alien topics of money and investing....and to find out what on earth the '*Footsie*' was!

Due to all of the constant tests and studying during Pilot training, I never really got round to properly looking at the world of Investments for another 18 months. But life was good. I was flying during the day, drinking and partying during the nights and every single penny I was earning was spent the moment it entered my account. So much so that when I was 19, I bought the new Mazda RX8.

Around that time I had another epiphany...funnily enough it was when I was accelerating through 130 mph down the centre of the runway at RAF Church Fenton. Now and again, after hours (*with permission of course*), I used to take a few mates in my new sporty car to razz up and down the runway trying to see how fast we could go. One summer's evening, one of my colleagues, Dave Reddy, was sat in the passenger seat and whilst we were setting up for another run he asked me how much my insurance was. When I replied, "£4500 a year", his mouth sort of exploded with spit. Now Dave is a really sensible guy. Really calm, never flustered, had a good head on him and was very tight with his money. And he really couldn't get over the fact that I had such a silly car with 6 points on my licence and that it was costing me £4500 a year to insure! I just shrugged it off as I hit the accelerator, but when we were halfway down the runway I realised that I really was a 'Class A' plonker. There was Dave, investing as much as he could every month for his future nest egg/house deposit and at the other end of the scale, there was me. Quickly realising how much of an idiot I was and that I would never be able to buy my own house at that rate. So it was then I realised that I really needed to increase my income...but how? I couldn't exactly ask the Queen for a pay rise and I really didn't have time to set up a part time business whilst learning to fly at the same time! So it was that night I started to slowly read up on everything money related and how to make a lot more of it! **This is where my money disasters began...**

Skip forwards 6 months and I was sitting in my room just Googling how to make more money. I was getting nowhere. My strict criteria was, 'How can I make money, on my laptop, wearing my PJs in bed...?' Online roulette and financial trading were the answers (*or so I thought*). I started with online roulette and figured that if I just kept betting on 'Red' and doubled up every time I lost, I'd eventually win. I mean, what are the odds of getting 'Black' like 10-15 times in a row? So I began and quickly made about £1500 in one night. I really thought I was the smartest guy on the planet and that I had it all figured out. I got a few friends in my room to prove what I was doing and quickly turned that £1500 to just over £3000. My head was sooooooo big. Then the inevitable happened. The roulette ball landed on 'Black' around 14 times in a row. I lost everything! My seed capital and my profits. The room went awkwardly silent and before I knew it, everyone had said their goodbyes. **This is where I made my first idiot mistake.** I got my credit card out and by the morning, I had lost just over £4000 with my credit card maxed out...

After licking my wounds and wiping the egg off my face, it wasn't long before I moved onto trading. I won't bore you with the details but long story short, I approached trading with possibly the worst attitude you could. The annoying thing is that I didn't learn a thing from my roulette calamity other than to never gamble again. So I really do cringe looking back at my younger self as I was far too cocky for my own good. I thought that if I could fly military aircraft, the world of trading would be a walk in the park! **Idiot Mistake No.2!** As a result, I did about a day of Googling to learn how to trade and then opened up a live £2000 account. I blew this account within hours! Did I learn from this? Nope. I did a bit more Googling, thought I had sussed it out this time, so I opened another £2000 account and lost that within a week! Some may say that there was a bit of progression there, but that really was an awful month for me!

Do I regret it all?

Not one bit! At the time I was inconsolable, but something in my gut was just telling me that I had to persist. So I did. Yes I had some hairy losses but there have also been some great profitable trades. The elation from making lots of money on your laptop whilst eating some toast, half naked is amazing; it really is. Now I'm not trying to put you off from trading or investing at all, but to highlight the point that if you treat the markets with zero respect, you'll lose money faster than you could ever do in a casino. Trading or investing without 100% knowing what you're doing and why you're doing it will always result in tears. And we don't want tears getting on your toast now do we? So even though I've made every mistake possible and spent years of clenching my fists and grinding my teeth together, I simply cannot express in words the amazing feeling of when it all finally clicks in your head. Knowing how to grow any amount of money by even 1% per month is just liberating. It's the single most important life skill to develop in my opinion and can only result in long lasting wealth if you do it properly. So my advice at this point is to really learn from all of the mistakes in this book and make sure you don't do them yourself! Just trust me when I say that when you finally become a profitable trader, you're going to have so much fun!

MISTAKE **1**: Day Trading

"Day Trading is the Devil." *For beginners*

96% of all traders lose money. It's a scary fact. The amount of traders emerging these days is increasing dramatically with the advent of cheap, fast internet connections, cheaper computers and free trading software. Even a shepherd in Mongolia could set up a live trading account on his iPhone. **But the reason why such a high percentage of people consistently lose money is because of Day Trading.** This is where you place dozens of trades per day (*if not more*) and close all of your trades by the end of the day. Also in order to Day Trade you typically need to spend hours per day with your eyes glued to your screen and by the end of the day, your eyes are exhausted and your brain is fried. Oh, and normally, your trading account will have taken a battering!

Trading is, and should be a life-skill, so Day Trading is a completely unsustainable activity in the long run as you'll either fizzle out mentally or you'll run out of money, or both. **Oh, and the stress!** Seriously, I have never ever experienced so much stress as I did when I was Day Trading large amounts of money and losing it! And I've been in some stressful situations like having emergencies whilst flying helicopters solo **and** I remember once I was flying a plane solo at night and I got lost. *(You've never really been lost, till you're flying on your own at night and you haven't the foggiest of where you are!)* For some reason, whenever money is involved, your heightened state of emotions just get amplified! This again is made worse if you're in a losing position but you kid yourself that it'll come back round, so you opt to let it run over night. Not a good idea. I promise you'll get the worst night of sleep ever. You'll just be checking your trades on your phone every half an hour and you'll be drained in every possible way which will make your next day of trading hopeless.

But even if you can manage all of that or you're not doing too badly *(everyone gets a winning streak)*, Day Trading is extremely hard to fit into your lifestyle. Most people have either a full time job or run their own business so you'll be working a minimum of 8 hours a day. In fact most business owners tend to work at least 10 hours a day. So where are you going to find the 3-5 hours a day in order to Day Trade? You can't...but if you do give it a go, I'm sure you'll eventually agree with me on this matter that Day Trading is extremely hazardous to your trading account and your health.

So if it's so bad, why does everyone do it then?! *(I hear you ask).*
Good question. It's mainly down to the internet and a distinct lack of information, education and training. What normally happens is people Google for information on how to trade and unfortunately, almost every single search result you will find is from a trading broker or trading training provider that promotes Day Trading. As a result, it's all people ever know. And the reason Day Trading is so heavily promoted is because of the commissions or spreads that are generated. For example, let's take the UK Stock Market, the FTSE 100. If let's say the price is 6790 and you want to buy it and 'go long' *(which means you hope it goes up)*, the price your broker will likely give it to you will be 6792. The spread *(the difference between those 2 prices)* in this example is 2 points. So your broker has immediately made 2 points in profit regardless of whether you win or lose your trade. So they obviously want people to make as many trades as possible so that they get more commissions and spreads. Therefore there are lots of commissions to be made which is why there are so many internet marketers out there promoting people to open up a live trading account through their affiliate link and to then get people to Day Trade. That way, every time someone places a trade, they get a kickback.

Siam's
Solutions

✓ **Avoid Day Trading like the plague.**

✓ Don't even entertain the idea that you are somehow different and that you can make it work. Even if you're a seasoned Poker player etc, I promise you that you won't. Day Trading should only be explored once you've got at least 3-4 years of successful trading under your belt. Otherwise it's like getting a 17 year old learner driver to race in the Grand Prix in an F1 car...it's going to end in tears.

✓ Most of the stuff you see on the internet about trading is just marketing or cons. So find someone who is trusted and respected and get tuition from them...so long as they are not teaching Day Trading.

✓ Day Trading involves looking at the 1, 5, 15 and 60 minute charts. **So remember this, anything below the 4 hour chart is just <u>noise</u>. You need to stick to the 4 hour, Daily and Weekly charts.**

Notes

MISTAKE **2** : Your Trading Seatbelt

"You wouldn't drive a car without a seatbelt, so don't forget your trading seatbelt"

When speaking with people that trade or 'dabble' in the stock market, I'm still shocked at how many of these people are completely unaware of what a stop loss is. For a beginner this is understandable, but for someone who risks their own money in the Stock Market, it's absolutely crucial one uses a stop loss.

What is it?

Well, when you place a trade or buy some shares, if for some reason there was some unpleasant news about your stock, it may suddenly plummet in price. And if this happened when you were asleep or away from your computer then you would lose quite a lot of money. Now a stop loss is your trading seatbelt. So let's say you bought some shares at say, £1 a share. You could set up your stop loss at £0.80 perhaps. What this means is that if for some reason that your stock were to crash in price, the moment it reached £0.80 a share, your trade would be instantly liquidated/sold. And as a result would have saved you a lot of money.

You can do this with absolutely any market whether you're trading stocks, currencies, commodities, bonds or other derivatives. It's one of the most important tools in your trading arsenal and those that don't use a stop loss will undoubtedly get burned at some point.

Also knowing where to put your stops is an art. Put your stop too close to the entry point (*The price you entered the trade*) and you'll get *'stopped out'* rather quickly. Put your stop too loose (*too far away from your entry point*) and it may as well not be there. Just like a car seatbelt. If it's too tight, it's too restrictive, but if it's too loose, you'll hit your head on the steering wheel. On my courses I show you exactly how and where to place and move your stop losses and it's a **crucial skill as you can use stops to lock in profit!** Yup, you read that correctly. Stops are not fixed, so you can move it up and down as freely as you wish. So let's say you bought a load of shares at £1 a share and it moved up in your favour to £1.50. You could move your stop loss up to say, £1.25. So if the market were to reverse, the moment it hits £1.25, your position would be closed. This means that you've locked in all the profit from £1.00 to £1.25. This is just standard practise just like putting the handbrake on when you park the car. So if you're not currently using stops....**use them.**

The £15k Pop Tart...

Ahh yes, those bloody Pop Tarts. My palms go all sweaty just reliving that moment. This all happened during my up and down years. It was during my first 2-3 years of trading and I was making some phenomenal profits one week and then the next week I would give it all back. I now know exactly what I was doing wrong and I'm positive that 96% of all traders are doing a mixture of these silly mistakes. Hence why I'm writing this book, but this Pop Tart Monday morning was probably the worst Monday I've had in my life. It was straight after a really good week of trading. The previous Friday I went back home to Norwich around £3-4k in profit for that week. It was a great weekend as a result of those profits and so my spirits were high as I started trading on that Monday morning. I was Day Trading (*so that's the first huge error I made*) and pretty much the first trade I placed went in profit almost instantly. Good start – I thought to myself. But my stomach was screaming for breakfast, so I quickly popped downstairs to put some Pop Tarts in the toaster, as you do. If you're a sweet-toothed junk food-lover like I am. Went back upstairs with my burning hot Pop Tarts and saw my trading screen alight with the colour of RED. Not a pleasing sight, especially as I had just placed a trade to go 'long' (*anticipating the market would go up*). But the market was just falling like a lightning bolt. I launched myself to grab the computer mouse so I could close the trade, but it was too late. Far too late. I closed the trade with a total loss of just over £15 000. I just sat there frozen with every negative feeling/emotion you could think of. It was utter gut wrenching to say the least. But the big error I made wasn't really placing the trade, **it was the fact that I didn't use a bloomin' stop loss!** And because of that, there was nothing protecting that trade in case it went wrong...that trade really ruined my week! So please learn from my pain!

Siam's Solutions

✓ **ALWAYS** use a Stop Loss. Every single time you place a trade, you need your stop in place. No one has a crystal ball and even if you've done every bit of research possible, you can still be wrong. With trading you can never be correct all of the time. Being a consistently profitable trader is all about risk management (*which we'll talk about later*), so your stop losses are the most important tool for mitigating risk.

✓ When your position gets into enough profit, move your stop loss up to break even (*the price where you entered your trade*) and so it then becomes a **totally risk free trade**. Then trail your stop up to lock in profit as the market moves in your favour.

✓ Always use a stop loss.

✓ See above... ☺

Notes

_____

_____

_____

_____

_____

_____

_____

_____

_____

_____

_____

_____

_____

_____

_____

_____

_____

_____

_____

_____

_____

_____

_____

_____

_____

_____

_____

_____

_____

_____

MISTAKE **3** : Emotional Trading

"Having emotions whilst trading is one of the quickest ways to blow your account"

Believe it or not, women make the best traders. Statistically speaking. It's common knowledge that women tend to be a bit more emotional than men in everyday life, however when it comes to trading, this is where women soar above men in this respect. You see, you absolutely must not have **any** emotions when you trade. Not one. You need to be in a frame of mind that has no greed, anger, frustration, ego, revenge and especially not excitement or hope. The reason being is that if you have any emotions, you'll trade in completely adverse ways. For instance, revenge. (*This is the most deadly of them all...*) If you've just lost a big wad of money on a trade, and you succumb to the revenge part of your brain, you'll begin to trade recklessly by trying to immediately 'win' back all of your money. You'll do crazy things like placing too many trades or even 'doubling-down'. Even a seasoned gambler would say that this is the worst thing you can do as it's just a downwards spiral of despair.

Now the peculiar thing here is that women are able to completely de-sensitise when it comes to trading. Ladies naturally tend not to have the big ego that's inherent with most men and so they don't let their emotions cloud their judgement. As a result, female traders are completely calm, calculated and methodical. They're also less likely to 'shoot from the hip' just because their gut is telling them to sell sell sell!

Siam's Solutions

✓ Don't trade if you're feeling slightly emotional. There shouldn't be any fear, hope, greed or anger. If your state of mind is anything other than calm neutrality, then don't trade. This may all sound silly but your mood really does reflect on the types of trades you place and you're more likely to stray from your Trading Plan (*more on this later*).

✓ If you do find yourself trading emotionally, immediately close your positions or at the very least, tighten up your stop losses in order to mitigate your risk. Then turn off your computer and go for a walk or do something else. For me, I just stick the Xbox on. Just do anything but trade.

✓ Remember that you need to be a cold, calm, logically thinking robot. If you watch Star Trek, Lieutenant Commander Spock is the perfect trading role model...

Notes

_____

_____

_____

_____

_____

_____

MISTAKE **4**: Over Trading & Boredom Trading

"Boring trading is good trading"

Over trading is always a standard mistake which every single beginner makes. Excitement and greed go hand in hand with trading (*as discussed earlier*) and more often than not, the result of this is to place far too many trades all at once or to trade all the time. Whether it's morning, noon or night they'll still be beavering away placing dozens of trades. Not only is this not a very good thing to do as you'll no doubt be losing money from either spreads, taxes or commission charges every time you place a trade, but it's hard to productively monitor all of those trades. And the amount of risk you're exposed to will most likely be quite high. Main reason is that a lot of the time someone will see something in the news like war is about to breakout so they'll hurry home to go and buy lots of oil/mining stocks, (*as oil tends to shoot up during times of war*), only to find out later that a peace treaty has been signed and then all of those stocks they've just bought have plummeted. And the trading account is hammered or wiped out.

Also, you really don't always have to be in a trade. This point took me a long time to get my head around. Your trading capital is sacred and so the No.1 rule of trading is **CAPITAL PRESERVATION**. Profits are just a bonus that comes with the activity. So with this in mind, you really need to be stringent in when and what you invest or trade in. Throwing as much mud at a wall and hoping some of it sticks is not a good method for preserving your capital.

Boredom trading is also a money-losing activity that people most likely do if they are also over trading. This will lose you money because if you're bored and you then go searching for something to buy or sell, you'll also most likely lower your standards when picking your trade. So long story short, if you're bored, don't trade and don't place trades 'just for fun'. It's for your own safety...

Siam's
Solutions

✓ Currency & commodity trading is slightly different, but if you do **trade** traditional 'stocks & shares', then the following is a good rule of thumb: If you have less than £5k, only have 1-2 stocks. £5k - £10k = 1-3 stocks. £10k - £20k = 1-5 stocks. £20k+ = 1-7 stocks. As in, if you had a pot of say £10k - £20k, try not to have more than 5 stocks at any one time. The important point to remember here is that this rule of thumb is only if you're **trading** these. Not **investing.** If you're investing in stocks and 'buying and holding' then of course, you can have as many stocks as you like. It's a debateable subject, but in my book, (*literally*), the key difference between trading and investing is time frame. If you're in and out within the space of 1- 120 days...you're trading, not investing.

✓ Don't '*spray & pray*'. You really must **never** be a machine gunner when you're trading. Placing loads of trades hoping something hits is not a good tactic. What you really need to be is a sniper. Snipers lay and wait until their target is in sight and then act. And snipers have a much higher hit rate than machine gunners. Trading is all about low risk/high probability outcome trades. You need to target the peachy low-hanging fruit, so when you see it, you take it. So remember, you need to be a sniper, not a machine gunner.

✓ If you're bored, don't go looking for trades.

✓ Try to limit the amount of trades you have on at any one time.

MISTAKE **5**: Dreadful Risk Management

"Risk Management is the SINGLE MOST IMPORTANT aspect of trading. Without it you are certain to fail every time you enter the market."

Combined with over trading and not using stop losses, poor risk management is one of the main reasons why so many people get chewed up by the markets only to quit and forever call trading 'gambling'. So if you ever hear someone calling trading gambling, they are either someone who doesn't know anything about trading or someone who's been hurt rather badly...or both.

Now one of the classic most common ways people practise poor risk management is by 'betting' too much per trade. For example, (*continuing on with the 'gambling' theme*), if you went to a casino with just £100 to play with and put it all on 'black', this is poor risk management. Main reason is that if you lose, you're out. And if you're out of the game, then you can't make any profits. This is an example of poor risk management in a basic form. Now let's say you wised up to this and returned the next day with another £100 but this time you only put £25 on black. Well, this is a lot better than before as it would take a few bad losses before you're 'out', but even this is still dreadful risk management as the **No.1 Objective with trading and gambling is <u>Capital Preservation</u>.**

It's quite interesting, in some of my seminars I ask the audience that if you had £5000 in your trading account and you were about to place a trade which you were confident about, how much of that £5000 would you risk? The answers always vary from £500 all the way up to £5000, but no one ever gets this question right. The majority of answers range around the £1000-£3000 area. Even the conservative people who say £500 are still far off the mark when it comes to risk management, because you just need 10 bad losses and your account is wiped! So the answer is.....£50! £50 is all you should risk on that trade. The unwritten rule of thumb all beginners **need** to stick to is the 1% rule. **Never risk more than 1% of your total capital per trade.** In fact, if you ask some experienced veteran traders they barely risk more than 0.5%. Regardless of how confident they are before entering the trade. I cannot stress how important this rule is and it's the single most important thing to remember when trying to **preserve your capital**. The reason being, if you were to lose 10 trades in a row, you would only be 10.48% down. This is easily recoverable. Now I hear a few of you thinking, *"that's way too small, I'll hardly make any money trading that small a position. I'll trade a little bit bigger to play it safe"*. Ok, how much bigger? Let's say 5% then. Well if you had 10 straight losing trades, instead of being 10.48% down, you'd end up being 40.13% down...that's a devastating blow to your account.

Another thing to think about with risk management is your RRR. Your Risk to Reward Ratio. Long story short, you need to make sure that your Rewards are at the very least **TWICE** that of your losses. I'll spare you the Maths, but what that means is that out of every 10 trades, you could totally lose 6 of them and you'll still be in profit. So just to repeat that, **you can have just a 40% success rate and still be in profit.** Not bad hey?

Siam's Solutions

✓ **<u>ALWAYS</u> stick to the 1% rule.**

✓ You need to try your absolute hardest to maintain a 1:2 RRR. I.e. Your wins need to always double your losses. In the long run, this 1:2 RRR will really look after you. One of the reasons casinos are extremely lucrative is that the odds are always in favour of 'the House'. In some cases, their odds are only a couple % in their favour, but it doesn't matter. It's a numbers game and in the long run the House always wins.

✓ Protect and preserve your capital like it's your only kidney.

✓ In order to stick with the 1% rule, you'll need to use your stop losses effectively. I.e. Set up your stops so that your trade is closed the moment you suffer a 1% loss. (*Specific details on how to do this would be too confusing in a book but I always ensure that this sound risk management is hammered into my students during the 2 day workshops*).

Notes

MISTAKE **6**: Wrong Mind-set Trading

"You are NOT going to make a killing today..."

What tends to happen when people start out, is that very early on, they'll have a winning streak. Whether it's beginners' luck or natural innate ability, **it's the worst thing that could possibly happen to you.** The reason being is that you will almost guaranteed think that you're 'Gordon Gecko' and are about to set the world on fire with your trading prowess. This, however, will nearly always lead to a catastrophic loss and you'll end up giving back all of your new profits and the rest of the money you started out with. I've done this 4 times! I used to think I was a smart individual back then, but now I just cringe when looking back at my younger self. If this has already happened to you, don't worry. **The best thing to do right now is to learn from your mistakes and find out why your trades went against you.** You'll probably find that you did a combination of mistakes I've written in this book. So don't ignore what happened and blame the markets. The markets are not wrong...you are. And what you're lacking is just the correct information, education and training. It took me a long time to figure that out. So hopefully this will now stop you from repeating this cycle another 3 times!

I've done a LOT of reading and listening of some of the best traders in the world, past and present, and one of the remarkable things I learned is that most of them actually feared the markets. With that fear, came a sense of respect for the markets and they knew that, like a minefield, one wrong footstep would ruin your trade or trading account. So the trick is to simply absorb as much knowledge and experience you can, and you'll eventually learn what a 'buried mine' looks like so you'll know exactly when and when not to trade. Now the knowledge bit is the easy part as you can read as much as you like. **But the experience part can only be developed through actual hands on trading.** Similar to flying a helicopter, you could know everything about helicopters and how to fly them, but until you've put in the hours of actual flying (simulator or real), you won't be able to hold a stable hover. But once you learn it, you'll never forget. Find any old aged pensioner who was a helicopter pilot and I guarantee you they'll still be able to hover if put to the test. (*Provided they still able bodied*).

So going back to the fear and respect one should have for the markets, it's important to be in the correct mind-set before trading. As previously mentioned, your state of mind should be **calm and neutral with absolutely no emotions.** But what I find quite handy which has been with me for years is a simple post-it note on my whiteboard in front of my trading station. It reads, "*Siam, today you're going to lose...and you're going to lose BIG*". This is probably contrary to what every Sports Coach/psychologist would recommend, as sportsmen and women absolutely need to go into 'battle' with a positive mind-set. But with trading, I guarantee that if you start your day of trading with a super happy, '*I'm going to make a killing today*' attitude, you'll lose...and you'll lose big. Or even worse, start the day with a monetary target you want to hit. What all of this will do is unconsciously make you place sub-standard trades or to overtrade in order to achieve your targets. So I guess that post-it note simply humbles me and prevents those horns of greed from emerging.

Siam's
Solutions

✓ If you do get a winning streak early on in your trading, first of all, congratulations! Trading is exhilarating when you're winning isn't it? Just please have the presence of mind to know that this streak isn't going to last for long and that you must always preserve your capital at all costs. So move your stop losses up to lock in some of your profits or at least break even. Also, re-analyse your trades to see what you did right.

✓ If you have already had the streak, got overconfident and have now subsequently lost everything, don't worry. Just really analyse what went wrong and treat the money that you lost as 'learning capital'. For me, my 'learning capital' was just over £50k as I was stupid and a slow learner at first. Don't follow in my haphazard footsteps!

✓ We all learn in 3 different ways. Visual, Audio and Kinaesthetic (seeing/hearing/feeling). So what you need to do is set up your 'VAK anchors'. You may already have these but you just don't know it. So what it is, is something Visual, Audio and something you can feel/do which puts you into the perfect trading mind-set. For me, I have a big whiteboard full of my goals, dreams and aspirations as well as a picture of the next car I want and a picture of the Earth from space (*one of my dreams is to spend a few days orbiting the Earth in zero-G*). These visual stimuli just reminds me of why I do what I do. Next is the audio anchor. Now I don't listen to classical music – ever, but there's a piano song called '*I Giorni*' by Ludovico Einaudi which completely levels me out. I don't know why, but I could be in absolutely any mood and this song just instantly returns me into a state of equilibrium. Very odd. Next is the kinaesthetic anchor. I've just got a squeezy ball on my desk and throwing it against the wall a few times whilst listening to the audio anchor does the trick. So now you just need to find your anchors. I never used to believe in this sort of 'stuff' but it really does work. This is why you'll see a lot of Traders working in the City wearing headphones whilst trading. They're just listening to their audio anchors...

✓ Never enter the markets with a monetary goal to accomplish for the day, week or month. It'll just adversely affect your trading. Plus some weeks there may not be a single optimal trade to place. Don't worry...the market just goes sideways sometimes. Your job is to wait and then pounce when the market starts trending.

Notes

_____

_____

_____

_____

_____

_____

_____

_____

_____

_____

_____

_____

_____

MISTAKE 7 : Buying Tips

"On the markets, peoples' wealth is being continuously transferred from the uninformed over to the informed. It's simply a case of knowledge which will stitch up those holes in your pockets..."

This is something that many 'dabblers' do. Basically anyone who says that they 'dabble' in the Stock Market, you can be 90% sure that they don't really know what they are doing and they are most likely losing money hand over fist. And 'dabblers' love to buy internet tips. Just do a search for trading or investing tips and Google will present you with hundreds of companies trying to sell you magazine subscriptions, expensive super snazzy software and email alerts all promising that their trade tips will earn you a fortune. Unfortunately you will be throwing your money away if you subscribe to any of these and will lose even more if you act upon the tips they give you. Now of course I'm getting out my big black tar brush here and I'm sure there are a few good ones out there, but what tends to happen is that the potential price movement has or is normally factored into the existing price. This is true especially for newspapers that have an editorial about a stock which is 'going places'. So when the masses pile into the new 'hot stock' etc, either nothing happens or it rises for a tiny bit before plummeting and taking all of your money with it. This is what's called a 'Pump & Dump' scheme. It's really prevalent and rife in internet forums and bulletin boards, especially the well-known and respected ones. So what happens is that a group of people pick a stock to target. They then heavily invest in that company which may start a bit of a rise but at the same time they will then launch a full scale internet campaign to ramp up the 'amazing sheer potential of this stock'. Thousands of naïve investors that don't know any better or how to actually do a proper stock analysis will then just blindly invest. The stock will then rise quite a bit (even better for the con artists if that stock is highlighted by a newspaper) and then when it reaches their desired price targets, they'll all at once sell their shares and close all positions. Before you know it, they've made a fortune and thousands of people are in extremely negative positions. It's an everyday occurrence in Penny Stocks and other stocks with low share prices. But you don't get any of this with currencies which is another reason why I predominantly trade the currency market as no man, group of people or company can influence the FX market (Foreign Exchange/currency) due to its sheer size.

Siam's
Solutions

✓ Do not under any circumstances buy anything online that promises overly great returns from tips or special strategies etc. These are just Internet Marketers, not proper traders.

✓ Avoid Penny Shares like the plague. I don't invest in the Stock Market (*for many many reasons*) but if I did, I would only buy stocks that were £10 or more per share. Main reason is that these types of companies tend to be going through the growth phase of their business and it's at this point (£10+) that major institutions start to pay attention. And if I'm going to put my money in a stock, I really do want big institutions to also invest as it's them that really drives prices up. Apple, Tesla and Netflix are prime examples.

✓ Continue to always learn and enhance your skills, knowledge and experience. Your BS detector will soon become finely tuned...

MISTAKE 8 : The Holy Grail Trading System

"Get Rich Quick Schemes DO NOT work. In reality they are Get Poorer Quicker schemes."

There are literally tens of thousands of different trading systems out there on the internet. Bucket loads. And each system or strategy has dozens of different variants. So what people tend to think to themselves is that out of that huge haystack of methods, there's bound to be that shiny needle which will pop their bubble of trading mediocrity and carry them to new glorious heights. As a result, these people will spend months and in some cases years of hopping from one method to the next without any real success. They may even get lucky and find a method that works for them for a month and then the next month it'll blow their account. So they'll move on. I've done this before (*thankfully not for too long*) and I've also spent good money on silly systems that seemed too good to be true.... and guess what? They were. So here's the upsetting blunt reality. **There is no Holy Grail Trading System. Fact.** So there's no point looking. The 2 industries with the highest amount of money and investment in the world are the Oil Sector and the Finance Sector. Oil is an obvious one as it's the blood of the world which is rapidly diminishing and so sexier technology is being created to locate and extract it, but the Finance sector is also just as big and lucrative. Banks and other private companies spend billions in research and equipment to find out how to leech as many pennies from the financial system as possible. So as a private trader at home on your laptop, you are competing against these behemoths and also some of the brightest minds in the world. As a result, we don't really stand much of a chance...unless you know what you're doing. But what these 'big boys' have found is that by using extremely fast internet connections and powerful computers, they can act in mere **nanoseconds** which means they can get in front of any move about to happen. They place millions of trades per day and so this practise is called High Frequency Trading (HFT). It's a huge grey area in a legal sense. Many parts of it are right on the cusp of the legal boundaries and some practises are about to be outlawed. For instance, one company called Virtu Financial (founded by Vincent Viola) is the King of HFT and in 1238 days of trading, they have had just **1 losing day. ONE!** This company makes on **average** around £1 million per day so this is about as Holy Grail as it comes.

Also the financial system has morphed into a completely different beast over the last 4 years. The markets are now changing roughly every 5 years or so. So a successful trading system in the 2000s is likely to be redundant today in 2014. This is why it's absolutely futile buying a method which you have no idea of how it works as you won't know when the best time to use it. Again, some strategies may work very well for Commodities, but not for Bonds or Stocks.

Siam's
Solutions

✓ Putting my preaching hat on again, but I really can't stress how important financial education is and if you are embarking on the trading journey, you need to actually know how and why everything works. Having more knowledge really is like getting a clearer lens in your glasses. So keep on learning and seek tuition from successful traders. You'll bypass years of frustration and lost money that way.

✓ Don't buy fancy expensive software or special trading strategies. You don't need special software as the free software you get with most brokers is sufficient. If a simple guy from Norwich can trade successfully and consistently with the free software on a laptop, so can you!

✓ Find a strategy which has a relatively consistent track record and stick to it. Again, the more knowledge you have the more accurate and decisive you can be when using it because knowing when and when not to place a trade or use a tool is crucial. If you want to learn what 4 methods I personally use, just visit my site and it will guide you on how to access these.

✓ Most scams/cons or '*buy this super-secret strategy*', these days are geared around Day Trading or Binary Options. **So stay away from both**. Anyone who tries to promote that you can earn between £100-£5000 per day is grossly misleading and will teach you how to Day Trade. This is where you spend hours a day glued to the screens and placing dozens of trades per day. Meanwhile, they will have hooked you up on their affiliate link so every time you place a trade, they get a kickback. It's absurd how many people are unaware of this. A safe guess would be 96% of traders. So remember, if you're being taught to look at the 1, 5, 15 or 60 minute charts...run away and don't look back. **This single tip will save you thousands.** I've learned the hard way. Day Trading requires hours of concentration on a daily basis. Which makes it totally unsustainable. I trade less than 5 minutes a day which is why I know I'll still be trading for decades to come, whereas Day Traders will get burned out in a monetary and mental exhaustion sense. Just try and find a Bank trader older than 30 years old...you won't. Most fizzle out by the age of 29!

Notes

_____

_____

_____

_____

_____

_____

_____

_____

_____

_____

_____

_____

_____

_____

_____

_____

MISTAKE **9** : Trading Bots

"Like a moth to a flame, people still keep buying them. It's just a product for marketers to sell. Trading bots are not a solution for trading laziness..."

Trading bots don't work. Simple. I fully understand why people buy them though. People have busy hectic lives and a demanding full time job, so they don't have time to trade or dedicate any time to learning. So when a sparkly new gizmo appears on an internet ad promising great returns whilst you leave the house for work, it can seem appealing. In fact that would be great in principle. A software that effectively turns your laptop into a trading cash machine whilst you eat, sleep and work. It's those same horns of greed that come out just like when deciding to buy the next '*Holy Grail Trading system*'. And if you start mentally spending the money you're going to make from this Trading Bot or fancy system...it's too late. You've already been sucked into the marketing.

So here's how it works. You either download a zip file or if the marketer is really snazzy, you'll get something attractive in the post like a DVD. You have probably already been upsold during the checkout process to buy the '*secret trading strategy*' that works best for this software. You then install it and press go. You'll then leave it running over night, wake up the next morning only to find out it hasn't really done much. Or you may even be in a slight loss. A key reason for this (other than this being a total gimmick) is that overnight, not much really happens during the Asian session for currency trading and absolutely nothing happens for Stocks. So you then give it the benefit of the doubt and leave it running all day whilst you go to work only to return home later to find 1 of 2 things:

i.) You've lost an obscene amount of money. Or,

ii. Not much has really happened and you've only lost a little bit of money.

In reality, the end result is the same. **You either experience the guillotine slicing of your account, or you just keep it running and slowly bleed your account with a thousand cuts.** Long story short, don't waste your time. Now here's the interesting part. That trading strategy the bot is using may actually be a pretty handy strategy and if you used it manually, you'd probably get better results. In fact one of my favourite strategies I use (*The Lambo Fund*) works terribly when you give it to a bot. But when I use it myself, that strategy alone consistently makes me over 20% per year. But the reason why the bot will always fail miserably is that it doesn't think. It just follows its set of instructions and only moves it stop loss up to the parameters it's set to. Whereas when you trade yourself, you will always be analysing the market and moving your stops to the optimum parts. Also, if you're a good trader, you will cut your losses short and let your winners run...trading bots can't do this as well as you can...

Siam's Solutions

✓ Remember, they are just a marketing gimmick.

✓ Don't waste your time or money.

✓ If you do insist on buying one (for an experience point of view or as an experiment), just set it up and only trade the smallest positions possible. So when the bot loses a trade, you only lose pennies or a couple of Pounds.

✓ Continue focusing on the things that really matter. Your knowledge, education and training...it's this which will result in your future payday and a life of disposable income.

Notes

MISTAKE **10**: Live Trading Rooms

"If you're trading the correct way, there is no need for live trading rooms. Day Trading is like Las Vegas. You get dazzled by the lights and potential riches, but most people leave Vegas poorer. Only the pros win..."

The internet is littered with Live Trading Rooms. **What are they?** They are simply webcams or screen-shares of a trader where you can *'look over their shoulder'* to see how they trade. They normally come with a monthly subscription of anything upwards of £50 and you'll be surprised at how bad some of them are. I remember signing up to one trading *'guru'* for 2 months and during those 2 months me and the other subscribers just sat and watched him in despair as he almost blew his whole account. Pretty much every trade he placed went against him and he always somehow managed to justify his trades. In fact, just for shits and giggles, if you're ever bored with time on your hands, try and find the cheapest and scammiest looking Live Trading Room you can find. This trader will no doubt be distinctly average to bad, but if you're lucky, you'll find someone like I did who is just plain awful. Then for fun, try putting some really small trades exactly opposite to what he's placing and see what happens. The reason I say 'he' is because I've never come across a female trader with a live trading room. Don't know why that is though...

Another reason why these are a waste of your time is because **you'll be watching a Day Trader**. And I hope I've hammered into you by now that **Day Trading is something you should avoid at all costs as a beginner.** Trading should be extremely mind numbingly boring. If you were to watch over my shoulder, all you'd see is me analysing all of the currency markets for 30 minutes on a Sunday night and that's it. You'd be bored for the rest of the week as I barely look at the markets other than on Sunday nights. But if I have live trades open, **I'll spend less than 5 minutes a day** monitoring them. I just glance at them on my phone just after I check my Facebook.

This is the only way how trading can effortlessly integrate into your life for decades to come. Day Trading won't.

Siam's Solutions

✓ Just don't waste your time copying/following a Day Trader. Regardless of how good he/she is. If they are genuinely good, it's because they've spent years learning their craft. You simply cannot effectively learn this in a year or less. Just like car racing, first you need to learn how to drive, then you need to learn how to manage spins etc and slowly work your way up to the F1 racing car. Skipping a few steps will likely result in a calamitous crash.

✓ Boring trading is good trading.

Notes

_____

_____

_____

_____

_____

_____

MISTAKE **11**: Email Updates

"Some of the best traders in the world read and subscribe to trading email updates only to take the opposite view..."

Just like shiny new trading systems, trading bots and live trading rooms, email updates from market 'gurus' are also just as common. From experience I've found that a lot of these updates are made from marketers who know a little bit about trading (*just enough to sound credible*), but when you ask a question, there is zero depth of knowledge. Just analyse the emails they send and there will no doubt be a link somewhere trying to get you to open up a live trading account through some broker.

There are some good ones out there, but you just have to be careful and please, whatever you do, don't blindly copy their trades! I've wasted thousands in the past from watching a video update etc and getting convinced that some currency is about to rise or fall, then without any of my own analysis, just go and place the trade. This has never ended well! So if you are convinced by an email or video update, just DYOR. (Do Your Own Research)!

Siam's Solutions

✓ Take these updates with a pinch of salt. If you've done my course you'll know exactly what to look for and whether the email/video is from a fraudster or not.

✓ Never ever place a trade blindly without doing your own research.

✓ I've done a couple of marketing courses myself whilst learning how to grow my businesses and there's an email tactic which is widely used by these trading marketers. It's called the 1 to 5 ratio. What they do is send you 5 really good value emails, then the 6th email will be a sales email. And so on. This is so that you begin to trust them before they hit you with a sale. From a marketing/business sense, this is actually a very good way to email your list. However when you finally receive the sales email, just properly analyse it for a bit. Is it a genuinely good offer or are they just trying to get your to open up a live account on their affiliate link?

Notes

_____

_____

_____

_____

_____

_____

MISTAKE **12**: Mainstream Media

"The Financial Times, Telegraph and the BBC are like the Sunday Sport to me. They only tell you what you want to hear...not the inconvenient truths you absolutely need to hear."

Pretty much every stat that the Government issues is grossly misleading and is close to plain lies. The main topics they totally mislead the public on are Inflation, GDP, Unemployment and Housing Data. So here are the bones of it all.

Inflation

According to the Government, UK inflation right now is 2.7%. Now this is the most farcical of all stats as it's becoming almost common knowledge that REAL inflation is near 10% now. The way they calculate inflation is by taking a metaphoric 'basket of goods' which the public buy from day to day like bread, milk, cars, iPhones and CDs etc. (*But funnily enough, not rent or houses. They used to, but they took it out of this calculation in 1983 as they started to purposely inflate the housing market*). So they just compare the prices of this basket to last month, last year, last 5 years etc and plot a graph. So right now they're telling us it's 2.7%. Well what they fail to realise or purposely ignore is that **everything** in that basket is now smaller or of less value than previous times. For example, let's take a Snickers bar (my favourite). In 2003, they were on average 30p. But now, they average around 60p. In fact I've spent around 90p in some places, so in 10 years, the price has increased by 100% minimum! AND they are all now 7.2% smaller. This same stat applies to everything else in the basket like packets of crisps, fairy liquid bottles you name it. So when you crunch the numbers, **real inflation** and **real living costs** are near double digits and are far outpacing economic growth.

Gross Domestic Product

Recently the US GDP calculations have been changed. They are now including Research and Development (R&D) spending as part of the GDP. Now this is absurd. The US spends more money on Military (R&D) than every country in the world combined. Even their medicine R&D dwarfs other nations. Now it could be argued that medicine R&D could produce more efficient medicines which would positively bring more revenue in, but it's negligible. Military R&D has next to no productive use (*other than for war*) and so this 'ploy' is something which will make the US Debt to GDP ratio not look as bad as it really is. They're the only country in the world to do this but it probably won't be long before the UK follows suit in order to hide our problems.

Jobs/Unemployment Data

This is a huge topic which I could ramble on for days, but in a nutshell, when calculating these figures, they are now purposely stretching the parameters of what a full-time employed person really is. They are now counting people with a 'part-time job but are seeking a full-time job' as 'fully employed'. They are including some forms of charity/volunteer workers as 'fully employed' and many other profiles. But they're doing it on the other end of the scale as well by classing some people without a job but are seeking employment as 'part-time' employed and so on. So they're trying to make these figures show that unemployment isn't as bad as it really is when the poor/rich divide is increasing dramatically! Just have a look at the BBC Documentary 'Skint' – it's shocking but a real insight into the UK's deprived areas.

Housing Data

Again, another topic which I could bore you on but this one is probably as laughable as the inflation data. For some reason the Government likes to promote to the public that a rising housing market means that the UK economy is improving. And as the public are grossly ignorant with investing matters, we just nod and accept what we see in the news. So 2 points here: i.) The housing market is NOT a reflection on how our economy is doing. **There is zero correlation between rising house prices equalling a better economy.** In fact, **rising house prices reduces GDP.** Main reason for that is because as house prices, mortgages and rent increases, it takes up a larger percentage of peoples' monthly income. As a result, if people are spending more on rent and mortgages, they will subsequently spend less in shops which therefore adversely affects our economy. **ii.)** The Government is now openly trying to pump up this market again with 95%

mortgages! Also when you look at US housing data that's even more of an exaggeration. What they fail to show us is that the Federal Reserve is buying up $85 billion a month of Mortgage Backed Securities, other toxic bonds and also at least 70 000 empty homes per **month** using proxies.

So there you go. Hopefully you can now see that we need to at the very least question what we are told. Housing, employment, GDP and inflation data is rigged which I hope I've demonstrated and that's only the tip of the iceberg. If they are rigging interest rates (LIBOR), imagine what else they are doing.

Siam's
Solutions

✓ So when you're next going to buy a mortgage, invest in the stock market or pensions etc, just please do a double check of REAL adjusted data, not nominal data which gets published. www. ShadowStats.com is a great site for real data...

✓ Try not to trade based on what you see in the news. Most of the time, the news has already been factored into the price of your market. This is why sometimes bad news comes out, but the market does nothing or even rises.

✓ Not really trading related, but if you're buying a house, be careful. Interest rates are at 300 year lows and they can and will only rise. This will have crippling effects to the economy and housing market. This is a huge topic which I cover in my other book, but what I'm strongly suggesting to my close friends and family is that they fix their mortgage ASAP for as long as possible!

Notes

_____

_____

_____

_____

_____

_____

MISTAKE **13**: Risk Capital

"You will 100% need some learning capital whilst you develop your trading skills and experience. Just don't expect to get your learning capital back!"

Everything has a price. And don't be fooled into thinking that the price is always in Pound Sterling. If you want to become a Master Knitter, the price will be most likely time in learning the skill and maybe a few bleeding thumbs. If you want to be a successful business owner or millionaire, the price you'll most definitely pay is time, lack of sleep, stress, diminished friend base and maybe a financial cost. You see the reason why a lot of people aren't millionaires or even wealthy is because they are not prepared to pay the price of becoming one. It's far easier to clock in at work for 8 hours a day, come home to dinner then go to the pub. Most of the population would shudder at the thought of quietly building up a part time business from 6pm to 10pm alongside their full-time job and managing their family. "*I just can't be arsed*" or "*It's just a bit too much effort*" or "*I don't have the time*" are comments I hear **all the time** from people who moan about their financial state but aren't prepared to grow out of their hole. But speak to any entrepreneur, stopping work for the day at 7pm would be an early finish! I know this from years of 12+ hour days 6 days a week! It just all comes down to your personal priorities and desire for gain. Take golf for instance. I like playing it with friends and of course, every time I play I always wish I was better. **Especially when you're constantly fading the ball into the bushes every tee shot.** But despite my desire to be a better golfer, I just have no inclination in doing what it takes to be a pro. I'm a '*fair weather golfer*' as I only like to play when the Sun is out and I absolutely loathe walking. So I guess I'll spend the rest of my life hoping I become a better player unless I eventually do something about it. Just like my friend Justin Fordham from JF Financial. He's the best mortgage advisor I know and he loves golf. He's already very good but he wants to be a pro. We played in a friendly competition the other day where he said his putting wasn't up to scratch, and he then said something which stuck in my mind for days after which is the inspiration for this chapter. He said he was going to go home and practise 2000 putts! Now that is dedication and I have no doubt he'll achieve his goal.

So getting back to trading, are you actually serious about becoming consistently profitable at it? **The ultimate reward from trading is that you will effectively turn your laptop into a cash machine and you can live the luxurious life you want with just 5 minutes a day of trading.** But are you prepared to take the time and effort in building your knowledge, the cost of doing courses to learn from successful traders, the 12 months in which it takes on average to become proficient and more importantly, are you comfortable with losing a small bit of your capital? The reason being that every trader that has ever lived has lost trades, lost money and has had losing streaks.

Siam's Solutions

✓ So it's best to get all of your learning and losing done early on. I always recommend that one stays on their simulation account until they are confident and profitable on it before opening a live £2000 trading account. But even still, I would treat that first £2000 as learning capital. Even expect to make mistakes and lose it all, but whatever you do, analyse every error and learn from your mistakes. **And even better, learn from my hiccups in this book!**

✓ Whenever you put money into your live account, this should be risk capital that you can 100% afford to lose. Please don't put your last Pound of next month's rent in your account. Yes, this is one of the silliest mistakes I've ever made and this will only result in a super-heightened level of anxiety and your trading performance will suffer! Big time...

Notes

MISTAKE 14: Penny Shares

"This is every naïve stock investors hunting ground. But for every Penny Share that hits the jackpot, there will be hundreds of thousands of stocks which will lose everyone's money."

We've all been there when we start out. Funds are normally tight so we naturally look for some cheap stocks so we can buy loads of shares. We think that the company only needs to rise a little bit and we'll make a killing. And as the share price is in the pennies, it hasn't got far to drop at all. This of course is all **WRONG!** I know it's alluring to go and buy a penny stock in the hope that the stock rises into the Pounds, but it rarely ever happens. Also even if you buy a share for 1p, it can still drop dramatically as the price can go into the decimal places like 0.001 of a penny. Plus if that stock goes bankrupt, you'll most likely lose you money. Bankruptcy or a stock market de-listing in the penny share arena is common. Plus huge spikes up and down are common.

There's also a very good reason why Penny Stocks or stocks on the AIM market (*the UK stock market for cheap stocks basically*) are so cheap, it's because a large majority of them are garbage. They are also the main staging ground for '*Pump & Dump*' schemes.

Siam's
Solutions

✓ For fear of sounding like a broken record, 2 things: i.) **Learn to trade and grow your financial education,** and ii.) **Don't even enter the stock market.** Especially at the moment with systemic risk being so high and the stock market grossly overvalued. The risks Wall Street are taking right now are 50% higher than that of 2007! I'm fully expecting a large Stock Market crash any time before 2017. Most likely in 2016. So right now I don't own a single stock. But I can trade the movement of them so this is why it's crucial that you learn how to profit when things go down as well as up. Also by learning how to trade properly you'll learn some valuable tools which will make stock picking 'simples' if you do intend on staying in this over-inflated market.

✓ If you do want to play in the Stock Market, try sticking to stocks over £10 as mentioned earlier.

✓ People treat these stocks like the lottery. So all in all, it's best to stay well away from Penny Shares and avoid bulletin boards and forums!

Notes

_____

_____

_____

_____

_____

MISTAKE 15: Mobile Phone Trading

"Trading on your mobile phone will burn a hole through your pocket quicker than a set of keys for a new car."

I can confidently attribute at least £26 000 worth of my losing trades in my first year down to trading on my mobile! I vividly remember one day I was on a train to London and was reading, what I thought at the time, was a bloody good trading email update. For some reason I just believed every word this 'guru' was saying and how the Euro was about to fall against the Dollar. So being the naïve newbie I was, I looked at the chart, it looked alright-ish, so I blindly followed him into this trade and sold the equivalent amount of about 1 million Euros. So I just opened up my trading app, punched in the relevant details and then began to watch my money run away like a wild horse! It was as though the whole market was waiting for me to enter, then as soon as I did, the market just rallied with big spike up after spike up after spike up. Within minutes I was about £6000 down. I should have killed the position instantly but like most beginners, I fell into the trap of relying on 'hope', wishing it would come back. So instead of cutting my losers short and letting my winners run, I let my loser run…and run and run…until I blew about £10 000 with that single trade! As you can see, I've made a fair number of the mistakes you've already read in this book on that trade, so please learn from my idiotic errors…

Upon further investigation, I realised that if I had my laptop and had looked at the chart properly, I would never have entered it. The picture the chart was showing was awful, but as my mobile phone's screen size was quite small (iPhone at the time) the chart wasn't showing me the full picture.

Siam's Solutions

✓ Always enter your trades from a laptop or computer. Never with your mobile.

✓ Do use your phone to monitor trades though. Closing losing positions or locking in profits with your stop losses is ok on your phone but just use it as a monitoring device...not a platform for analysis and placing trades!

Notes

_____

_____

_____

_____

_____

_____

_____

_____

_____

_____

_____

_____

_____

_____

_____

MISTAKE **16**: Snatching

"Without doubt the hardest thing __not__ to do..."

Snatching at profits is something you will 100% do. No matter how blunt I am in this chapter or how long and detailed this chapter is, I know for a fact that you will at some point ignore or forget my warnings. It's just human nature. As I said previously, you need to let your winners run and cut your losers short. This all stems back to sound risk management and risk to reward ratios, but you **really** really do need to let your winners run. It's these runners that will completely offset all of your losing trades, and then some. I tend to make about 3-15% per month, (around 3-7% on average) but every now and then, because I'm a trend trader, I will latch onto a trend and ride it to its full extent. Sometimes a single trade will return me 10%+. Also at least once a year I normally get into a trade which will make me 30%+. So this is why you need to let your winners run.

However, I can fully understand how hard it is to resist that snatching urge. Whether you close the trade to realise the profits or move your stop loss right up close to the market price in order to lock in as much profit as you can, **just resist!** For instance, let's say you're in a trade which is now £5000 in profit...every single bone in your body will be screaming at you to lock in say £4000, or even £3000. **Just resist!** You need to completely ignore the monetary value of the trade and place your stop loss according to the teachings you have learned. **I personally still struggle with this sometimes.** It wasn't long ago I was in a trade which was about £12 400 in profit. It was a beautiful US Dollar/Chinese Yuan trade and I was shorting it (*essentially betting that the US Dollar would go down*). It was a really nice downwards trend which I was riding...then very quickly my profits jumped from about £8000 to £12 400 (there was a spike down). My whole body was yelling at me to lock in the profits, but I had to just resist and leave my stop loss where it was. The probability of it rebounding back was high, so I stayed put. A few days later, it rebounded back and then kept on falling. If I had snatched, I would have missed out on the subsequent continuation of the trend...

 *Siam's* **Solutions**

✓ Stick to your training on where and how you move your stop losses.

✓ Try your hardest not to snatch.

✓ If you are going to snatch, definitely make sure you're not snatching at a profit which is below your 1:2 risk to reward ratio. I.e. You need to keep your profits at a minimum above twice that of your expected risk on that trade.

✓ Once you place your trade, get rid of the screen that shows you how much money you're up or down. Just look at the chart and stick to your training.

Notes

_____

_____

_____

_____

_____

_____

_____

_____

_____

MISTAKE **17** : <u>News Trading</u>

*"Unless a **<u>huge</u>** catastrophe has occurred like a freak earthquake or nuclear bomb has gone off, do not trade the news!"*

You see on films and TV that the typical trader has a big screen with the news constantly on so that they will be the first to hear of any breaking news and then they can profit from that news on the markets before the masses can react. **This I'm afraid is a load of tosh.** And I'm pretty sure that those who emulate this sort of trading don't do too well!

As you now know there are giants in the markets like Banks, Central Banks and HFT companies. These big boys are placing millions of trades per day and they also have super-fast links so that if something does happen in the news, they hear about it first before anyone else. And as they act in mere nanoseconds, the price will have always moved by the time you see it and react to it.

However, if something huge and horrible has happened, then the various markets are going to rise and fall. A recent example is with the Japanese earthquake. This was a no brainer trade as it was obvious the Japanese Stock Market and the Japanese Yen would spike down...it did. But you have to be careful because after sharp moves like this, the market nearly always rebounds or 'snaps back'.

Siam's
Solutions

✓ Just avoid trading news events. Remember, you are a sniper, not a machine gunner, so just keep to your low risk high probability outcome trades. It's those low hanging fruit trades where you make your money...

✓ If something big happens, you need to act very quickly...but tread carefully and watch that market like a hawk!

✓ Another popular news trading event would be whenever the US announces their unemployment data (Non Farm Payroll) or whenever the Federal Reserve issues statements. Stay well away from these events. If you have open trades, just tighten up your stops as the market goes wild. This erratic price movement happens every month like clockwork!

✓ To find out when these big news announcements are issued just Google 'Forex Calendar' and there you go.

Notes

_____

_____

_____

_____

_____

_____

MISTAKE 18 : Multiple Trades

"You're not a circus juggler..."

We've already talked about boredom trading, overtrading and poor risk management but having multiple trades open at the same time is nearly always the **result** of those previous mistakes. Just to clarify things, when I was talking about overtrading earlier, that's relating more to trading all the time or trading in unsuitable hours. Whereas this chapter is focusing on having many trades all open at the same time. There's no set rule for this, but the way I see things is that **you never really want to have more than 5 trades open at any one time.** The main reason is that the moment you go over this number and have say 10 trades open, monitoring and managing them becomes a handful! Let's say something happens on the markets and all of a sudden you have 5-10 trades all reacting differently. Some may be plummeting and some may be rising. So by having more trades open than normal, you'll find it hard to react properly and cut a loser short etc. I once gave some 1 to 1 private tuition to a person and he had 19 trades open! 19! The internal risk management alarm in my head just exploded...I literally struggled to speak for a few seconds...

Also there's the exposed risk to think about. Even if you've followed my advice and stuck to the 1% max risk per trade, if you have 10 trades open and they all go against you (*it can happen*) then all of a sudden, you're 10.48% down! Not a good day at the office!

Siam's
Solutions

✓ There's no hard and fast rule, but what I personally do is try to have a maximum of 5 trades open at any one time.

✓ As well as the 5 trades rule, you really do need to limit your total risk/exposure. So if you have 5 trades open, make sure that you're not risking more than a total of 3% of your total capital. So in this case, if you have 5 trades open, then each trade needs to be risking no more than 0.6% each.

✓ Trust me, you really don't want to be losing more than 3% of your capital on any single day...and if you do hit your 3% loss limit, just stop trading. Turn the computer off and comeback tomorrow with a fresh mind. Whatever you do, **DO NOT TRY AND WIN ALL OF YOUR MONEY BACK STRAIGHT AWAY!**

Notes

_____

_____

_____

_____

_____

_____

_____

_____

_____

MISTAKE **19**: Choosing Your Broker/Trading Platform

"This is a large murky grey area which I'm surprised that some of the activities that some brokers do aren't outlawed!"

Before we start, I need to explain the difference between a broker and a trading platform. The broker is the company that you set your account up with and they facilitate all of your trades. The trading platform is just the software that you use. But most of the time, your broker will have their own trading platform. But some brokers will just get you to use a generic universal trading platform.

This chapter may make the difference between frustrating stagnation and success with your trading. I spent the first 2 to 3 years trading with a trading provider/broker who I thought was quite good. I liked their software, the charts were good and in general it was just a nice and intuitive platform. However I really wasn't getting anywhere. I was winning big, losing bigger, had a few winning months and more losing months.

So after 3 years of trading I actually considered myself to be quite a knowledgeable trader due to my unquenchable thirst for knowledge and information...but I was barely making a profit or even breaking even. I felt lost in my state of continuous frustration and was clueless as to what to do. Then one day I got a random cold caller from another trading provider who was trying to coax me into opening up an account with them. The young chap explained all of the pitfalls of my broker and said that theirs was better due to a number of different reasons. Obviously I was dubious as it appeared to be just general sales chat, but he did get me thinking. And what he was explaining to me was that there's a big difference between trading platforms/broker. So out of curiosity I gave in and opened up a live account with just £2000 to give it a test drive. **The results were**

remarkable. All of a sudden I was pretty much a trading God! (*In my excited mind at the time anyway*). Over the next few months, my consistent trading success rate just soared for the 1st time in years yet I wasn't doing anything different. But then one day I got the Euro-Dollar chart open from both brokers and the chart was different. The old broker I was with had random spikes in price all over the place. Yet on the chart of the new software, there were a lot fewer. No wonder I wasn't doing well on the old platform, these erroneous spikes were the reason I was always getting stopped out of a trade! This perplexed me and so after some in-depth research, what I found shocked me.

There are 2 main types of brokers. **MMs (Market Marker) or ECNs (Electronic Communication Network)**. This can get a bit technical, but long story short, if your provider is a MM, whenever you place a trade, your trade goes directly to them, then they decide whether to pass on your trade to the market. But if an ECN is your provider, whenever you place a trade, it goes directly to the market. So in essence, the Market Maker is your middle-man. Now this gets interesting because these MMs know exactly how good each one of its clients are at trading. So they essentially categorise their clients into 'bad traders' and 'good traders'. So when a bad trader makes a trade, the MM will get that trade and just absorb it knowing that this person is a bad trader and normally loses. So this trade never actually reaches the market. The MM is now effectively betting against you. So when this happens, if the trader does lose the trade, all of losing money goes straight to the MM. Vice versa. However when a good trader places a trade, the MM knows that this person is normally correct, so they will then place that trade into the live market. That way the MM doesn't lose or win anything other than their commission or spread from the trade. Now this is being looked at in a big way and so MMs are now making a lot of effort in their marketing material to say *"We don't go against you in your trades"*. Unfortunately, 90% of brokers out there are MMs and they'll lure you in with really sexy software and low spreads. And low spreads is exactly what you need if you're a Day Trader which is exactly what MMs want as that's where all of their juicy commission is.

Not only that, there's a lot of controversy about '*Stop Runs*'. Basically, as a MM, they can look at a stock or currency pair and see where everyone has put their stop losses. So some MMs have been known to manipulate the market or charts or spreads so that everyone is taken out 'stopped out' before letting the market continue...As I said before, this whole chapter is shrouded in suspicion, controversy and opaque information...

How do you know if your broker is an ECN or MM?

Just Google the name of the broker, followed by 'market maker?' For instance, let's take the broker IG Index. All you need to do to is to Google 'IG Index market maker?' You then need to find the search result which is from a forum. 9 times out of 10 you'll straight away see whether it's a MM or ECN. And to save you the time, IG Index is a MM...

Siam's Solutions

✓ Use an ECN broker. I set all of my students up on an ECN provider. This way you can just get piece of mind knowing that no one is going to 'Stop Run' you or take the other side of your trade.

✓ If you do use a MM, just place your stop losses a bit looser than normal to be safe...

✓ Not many people know about the information within this chapter so I'm probably not making many friends in the MM community any time soon...

Notes

MISTAKE **20**: Taking Advice

"Would you ever take dieting advice from an obese binge eater?"

Taking investment advice from poor people is an interesting topic because everyone does it. The other day I thought I'd have a reminiscent gander over my trading/investing diary. I'm gobsmacked at some of the risks and dodgy trades I placed in my first year but hey, find me just 1 person who set the world alight during their first year in the markets! But the curious thing which stood out the most is that I've got a red star marked next to every time I've taken someone's advice to not do something. I call it my 'missed opportunity star' and it illustrates a very important reminder that who we take or don't take advice from is crucial to your finances! For instance, would you take fitness advice from a 20 stone binge eater? No... then why on earth would you take financial advice from someone who's financially illiterate? Or investment advice from someone who doesn't invest with their own money?! This is why I have a strict rule that **I only take business advice from successful business owners, investment advice from successful investors and general pensions/wills/trusts advice from IFAs.** You see most of my red stars are from occasions where I've listened to either a friend or an IFA to not invest in something, only to find out that their advice was grossly wrong and I've missed out on a winner. This is why I **never** take **investment advice** from IFAs, accountants or solicitors. Statistics show that a huge majority of the people in these professions don't invest with their own money and nearly all of them just earn a living from their 9-5 wages as opposed to returns from their investments.

Siam's Solutions

✓ The next time your friend, newspaper article, parent, stock broker or anyone tells you that a stock/commodity/investment product is a winner/loser, just do a double check to see how that person makes their money...

✓ Developing a keen sense of discernment or a BS detector will hopefully keep you out of trouble!

✓ If you insist on jumping into something on a 'tip', at the very least, risk very little of your total capital!

Notes

_____

_____

_____

_____

_____

_____

_____

_____

_____

_____

_____

_____

_____

MISTAKE **21**: Research Bias

"You need to discard your pride in investing and trading. Don't feel as though you have to always be correct in your market opinions otherwise you'll fool yourself into making costly decisions"

Back when I was 19 and starting to 'dabble' with Penny Shares (*yes, we've all been there!*) I remember a share tip from a friend. He said that I really needed to buy Desire Petroleum shares. Being new to all of this and trusting him as he seemed knowledgeable I bought some DES shares with minimal research. After a month, my shares were up by about 10% - I thought I was Gordon Gekko! So I bought more...and more. To be honest, I became a little bit obsessed with this company and was reading all sorts of things about the company on trading forums, trading websites and journals. In fact it got to the stage whereby I was actually quite delusional about DES and thought that this share could only go one way – up. But the more I researched I kept finding things which contradicted my *'bullish'* opinions. **But I just dismissed it.** In fact I remember being so biased towards DES that I discarded an important bit of information about the company's debt, which, if I had seen this bit of evidence with a clear head, I would have immediately exited from that stock. But I didn't. I only **saw what I wanted to see.** As a result I lost over £1500. This was a big loss for me at the time.

Siam's
Solutions

✓ So the big lesson I learned here is that with investing, one should be like a Vulcan (from Star Trek). Be systematic, logical, have no emotions or attachments to your investment and know that there may be a huge piece of the puzzle you're missing! So now, before I even consider any investment, all I do is actively search for reasons not to invest and to always remain objective. Believe it or not, even now, I still actively investigate reasons to not invest in Silver and Gold...I'm still looking...

✓ You need to be 100% flexible with trading and investing. Just because you thought or said an asset was going to go up, the moment you realise you were wrong, you need to either exit your position or in fact reverse it. Notable Billionaires like George Soros have been completely wrong on the news several times now, but they are always the first to admit their error and will react accordingly.

Notes

_____

_____

_____

_____

_____

_____

_____

MISTAKE 22 : Indicators

"If your chart looks like spaghetti, you are likely to fail"

When new traders start out, they eventually read up on indicators. Just like I said that there were thousands of trading strategies, there are also thousands of different chart indicators. Bollinger Bands, Stochastics, MACD, Fibonacci, Parabolic SAR and Moving Averages to name a few. Ultimately, every indicator is just a bunch of squiggly lines reporting all sorts of information like whether the market is overbought or sold, whether the market is trending etc. So the common pitfall here is to load up your chart with lots of different indicators. Like more than 3. This results in a very messy screen and you'll be obscuring what the market is actually doing. When you're looking at the charts, all you should really care about is Price Action. **I.e. What has the price done? What is the price doing now? And with the patterns that form from the lows, highs and movement of the price, what is the price likely to do in the future?** That's all you should really care about. Indicators can be a big distraction if you're not too careful so don't let them overcome you!

Siam's Solutions

✓ If you have a good trading strategy then it shouldn't have
more than 3 indicators. So you should be fine. If you don't have
a specific strategy, just try not to have too many indicators
otherwise you'll suffer from analysis paralysis as some indicators
will contradict others and you'll end up not placing trades or
placing bad ones!

Notes

_____

_____

_____

_____

_____

_____

_____

_____

_____

_____

_____

_____

_____

_____

_____

_____

MISTAKE 23: Scalping

"Imagine Day Trading on steroids...that's Scalping..."

Day Trading gets you to predominantly look at the 5, 15 and 60 minute charts. As you now know, you spend hours glued to the screen and you're more likely to place higher leveraged trades etc. Well Scalping is the adrenaline junkie's version of Day Trading. Here you'll be looking at the 1 minute chart and placing trades that last from a few seconds to a few minutes! Oh, and you'll be placing loads of trades! In the space of 2 hours, it's not uncommon to see people that have made 30-50 trades.

Now just like Day Trading, Scalping can be an effective way to trade if you're a very skilled trader with years of experience under your belt. And I know some very successful people that do Scalp and Day Trade, but they know what they're doing. Just like putting a random person into a fast jet and getting them to land on their own...that would just end in disaster. But for a fighter pilot, it would be a doddle! Unfortunately the public's sentiment on trading has been completely tarnished by the droves of beginners that lose everything trying to do one or both of these riskier trading activities...

Siam's Solutions

✓ Trading doesn't need to be time consuming or stressful. I trade less than 5 minutes a day...I'm a pretty chilled guy. Not when I was Scalping though!

✓ Avoid it at ALL costs. Don't even entertain the thought of doing this...ever.

Notes

_____

_____

_____

_____

_____

_____

_____

_____

_____

_____

_____

_____

_____

_____

_____

_____

BONUS MISTAKE:
Your Trading Plan/Journal

"Building a house without following a plan may result in wasted time and money. The same principle applies to trading."

Now and again, whenever Ellie (*my lovely wife*) and I have dinner in front of the TV, the program Grand Designs always seems to be on at the same time. So we watch it and I'm amazed to see how many homeowners blindly jump into their huge property reconstruction without any blueprints or plans/advice from architects. They just do it on a whim and nearly every episode ends with the homeowners overspending by a large amount and the project tends to have taken longer than anticipated. To me, it's just inconceivable that I'd embark on such a huge task without consulting the professionals and planning out where every nail goes. But this same haphazard approach applies with trading. I'm a prime example of this when I started out. **So you really do need to have a detailed plan before you start trading.**

Now I've met a lot of traders in my time. Lots of good ones and even more bad ones. The good ones are hard to find, as successful traders tend to be isolated and low key. They trade because they love it and they don't really have much of an ego. In the very good book 'Market Wizards' there's a chapter where a trader called Brian Gelber was being interviewed. In this interview he was talking about the big 1987 market crash and that in the newspapers there was this alleged super trader who made $20 million from the crash in just 2 weeks. This 'super trader' had loads of press coverage for weeks and he seemed to love it. But Brian quietly made around $20 million in 20 minutes during this time. Yet this guy is completely unheard of. So too are the other handful of traders within the Market Wizards book. I'm digressing here, but what I've found in my travels is that **the single tool/habit that differentiates good traders from the rest, is the adherence of a strict trading plan and trading journal**. And Brian is very strict about his journal.

Most retail traders (*private traders like you and I*) fail in this arena because they either treat it like a lottery/casino or they treat it like a hobby. Unfortunately, if you treat trading like a hobby, you'll get hobby-like results. So you really do need to treat this like a business and 2 of the main ways you can do that is by trading within the parameters of a strict trading plan (*so this forces you to just take the low hanging fruit*) and also by keeping an accurate log/journal of your activity/results. You see for most people this is too much of a 'chore' and so they eventually end up giving up. I recently lost over 3 years' worth of trading logs in my last house move...I'm still properly gutted by this.

Siam's Solutions

✓ Treat this like a business and be disciplined to only trade in accordance of your trading plan.

✓ Maintain a journal/log of all the trades you place. You can either keep an electronic spreadsheet with all of your profits, losses, entries, exits, max risk and reasons why you entered/exited the trades etc. However I prefer using a slightly old fashioned paper approach. My mind prefers pictures and graphs rather than spreadsheets, so every time I open a trade, I take a screenshot of the chart and then digitally write on the chart the reasons I entered. (*I just use Microsoft Paint*). Then when the trade is finally closed, I take another screenshot and doodle over that. I then put the 2 screenshots onto the same page and then print it out. This A4 printout then goes into a folder. Over time this folder becomes a treasure chest of information and analytical data. You'll be able to identify all sorts of trends or habits which lose you money. It really is the best way to maintain a log, despite the paper and ink costs!

Summary

So I hope this quick broad brush overview of every mistake I've ever made helps you in some way. Even if you're already an experienced trader, I'm sure there's still at least 1 nugget which you can take away from this which will help your future profits.

I'm extremely passionate about trading and investing as it really is a way to escape the Rat Race if you treat it properly. I say to people that if you take this slow and steady and not try to make silly% per month, you'll develop this into a life skill which will eventually enable you to semi-retire or even fully retire in a fraction of the time that people in the Rat Race will.

Unfortunately we get indoctrinated from our parents and schools that you need to do well in school, get a good job and then retire on a big fat pension. Whereas in reality that very rarely happens. **Those days are long gone.** I call the Rat Race the **40/40/40 Plan.** It's where you work 40 hours per week for 40 years and then retire on a pension 40% of what you struggled to live on in the first place. **That, in my opinion, is the worst financial plan one could ever do, yet it's what most sign up to.** But financial trading really is a good way to escape this, it really is. I'm confident most people could semi-retire in just 10 years or even 5 years if done properly. Treat this as your DIY Pension. Now for those that know me, the word 'pension' to me is like garlic to a vampire. The state pension really isn't worth the paper it's printed on! I could go on, but in a nutshell, **if you wanted to retire on a pension of £2000 per month, you'd need a pension pot of half a million Pounds.** That's a contribution of **£1000 per month for 40 years!** Extremely unattainable for most! But in order to get the same result from trading, assuming a realistic performance of 2% per month, you'd need just £100k in your trading account. Now £100k may seem like a lot of money and unattainable for most people as well, but it's certainly a lot more achievable than the standard pension or the common perception that you need 'millions in the bank' in order to retire or semi-retire. The reason I say this is because when you get to the point whereby you know 100% deep down in your gut that you can grow your account by at least 20% per year or 2% per month, you're already halfway there.

Also the secret weapon for the world's best investors and traders is compounding interest. Here's a table to illustrate this:

Example of Compounding Interest in your Trading Account with a performance of just 2% per month

STARTING CAPITAL	£10k	£20k	£10k + £250/m
END OF YEAR 1	£12,682	£25,365	£15,725
END OF YEAR 2	£16,084	£32,169	£23,296
END OF YEAR 3	£20,399	£40,798	£32,897
END OF YEAR 4	£25,871	£51,741	£45,075
END OF YEAR 5	£32,810	£65,620	£60,519
END OF YEAR 6	£41,611	£83,223	£80,106
END OF YEAR 7	£52,773	£105,546	£104,947
END OF YEAR 8	£66,929	£133,859	£136,451
END OF YEAR 9	£84,883	£169,765	£176,405
END OF YEAR 10	£107,652	£215,303	£227,078

Now getting to the point where you will be consistently making 2% per month is very realistic but it will take at least 12 months to get to that point. But as you can see from the table, in just 10 years you will have built up a large enough trading account to generate at least £2000 per month. And unlike a pension, your capital doesn't dwindle away as you withdraw from it. The reason I've highlighted the end column is because this is the scenario which I'm always confronted with. I'm continually meeting people who have £10k wasting away in some savings account and they're also paying into a workplace pension etc. **Well if you started to learn how to trade and got yourself to the confident position of making 2% per month, you can then start your own DIY pension knowing that you'll amass over £200k within 10 years.**

But here's the exciting bit. As time progresses, you'll find that your skills improve and so your returns may be between 2-5% per month. **That's when this becomes really exciting.** If you started with £10k and added £250 per month like with the last column but made 3% per month, after 10 years your pot would be around £619 610.

What to do now then?

Obviously my advice would be to start learning how to trade as soon as possible regardless of what career/profession you're in or whether you're a struggling or successful business owner. **I strongly believe that most people need to learn how to trade the currency market as it's a life skill.** As I said earlier, as long as there are humans around, there will always be a currency market. So if you know how to trade this market, you'll always know how to profit from it. Also there's roughly 1 global market crash every 7 years and these market crashes are the easiest time to make money. It's quite common to see a single trade make you over 30% ROI. This is why traders love market collapses. It's just the best time to pounce on some extremely low risk high probability outcome trades! So here's a suggested route to follow:

1. Make the conscious decision that you want to learn how to trade properly and **commit to it**. There's no point in starting this if you are going to treat it like a New Year's Resolution fad like getting a gym membership and then never going to the gym.

2.) As it will take you around 12 months to become proficient, start to learn now. Not tomorrow, but now. And don't let the old excuse of 'I *haven't got any time*' get in your way. My 2 day trading course fully equips you with everything you need to know to get started and trading will only take 30 minutes on a Sunday night and less than 5 minutes a day! Anyone can integrate that into their lives.

3.) Book yourself onto the next course at www.TheRealisticTrader. com

But how much money do I need to actually get started!?

It's a great question, I'm glad you asked! ☺ Not as much as you probably think. You don't even need your £10 000 anytime soon. So here is a realistic breakdown of the start-up costs:

- £997 for the intensive 2 Day workshop
- £500 for 1 year membership for on-going follow up support (can pay monthly)
- £200 for the hotel overnight costs
- £60 fuel for travelling to and from the workshop
- £20 for the dinner that we have at a local restaurant on the first night of the course.
- £2000 starting capital after 3-6 months of simulation trading.

So all in all, you'll need £3777 over the first 6 months and just £1777 straight away to get going.

I hope that this has helped you in some way or another so I bid you farewell and please feel free to share and pass on the knowledge you've learned in this book. I'll leave you with 2 quotes that have looked after me for years:

"Stop building someone else's dream and start to build your own"

&

"The <u>ONLY</u> failure in life is to give up or not pursue your life goals, dreams and aspirations!"

Some reviews on The Realistic Trader 2 Day Intensive Trading/Investing Workshop:

"Wow...I used to do a bit of trading in the past and I've spent a fair amount of money on other trading courses before and this Realistic Trading course is hands down the best course I've seen. It is extremely realistic, Siam doesn't up-sell you other products on the course and he doesn't try to sell you the dream. Whether you trade or have no interest in trading you need to do this course. It's so much more than trading! What a genuine guy and a great teacher and trader. Thank you Siam, top stuff!"

– Terry Gormley – Director – Unlocking The Will To Act

"Without a doubt, Siam is the leader in this industry with detailed, clear and relevant content that is 100% ready for implementation. I will be recommending all of my family and business colleagues to take this course! This should be taught at school!"

– Richard Dwyer – Director – Flair

"I have wanted to master FOREX for a long time. Previously I paid for a course and learnt Day Trading strategies. Not only was I not succeeding, the task of sitting in front of a screen all day was too tedious. After Siam's course I can now place safe trades in less time. Siam's teaching style is easy to follow and I'm excited to now place some trades."

– Su Augusta – Director – Luxx London

"Excellent. Huge knowledge base presented in a simple fashion. I would highly recommend the course and Siam to my peers."

– Richard Williams – Director – Righteous Aviation

"Came into the course with no background knowledge but with a masterplan to earn some cash. Siam catered for all levels of experience/expertise and never left a question unanswered. Of particular impact was how not to trade

as Siam allows everybody to learn from his mistakes (saving us years of pain)! Left the course confident in starting a 3 month practice account that will result in good profits."

– Ben Whittaker – RAF 'Royal Squadron' Pilot

"A new skill learnt in a weekend but will stay with me as a life skill!"

– John Davy – Founder – The Jongleurs Comedy Club

"Trading can be a minefield. No different to most things in life. However you are taught the simple disciplines and given correct guidance, you quickly realise that trading is not that difficult. Just like writing or driving. Perfect course and well delivered!"

– Justin Fordham – Director – JF Financial

"Great course, hands on practical experience of the strategies used. Would highly recommend!"

– Ram Jeyarajah – Doctor

"I come from a financial background (accountant and having worked in an investment bank). However I found the course insightful and provided me with a basis for getting going straight away (albeit with a dummy trading account). Siam's style is engaging, interesting and informative. Thanks and looking forward to using a new life skill!"

– Ben Fells – Chartered Accountant

"After a solid two days on the Realistic Trader course I've moved from a basic novice to being confident that I understand FOREX enough to enter the markets and start placing trades. I've learned a life skill in 2 days that 99.99% of people do not know of and I can't wait to put it to work!"

– Rob Taylor – Recovery & Insolvency Solicitor/Consultant

"I was never interested in FOREX because I've been in property for 10 years but when I saw Siam and his approach, I was interested. The course was full

of content and no upsells. Core methods to use and realistic targets. I'm now confident in my new ability. Thanks Siam."

– Lawrence Nisbett – Property Investor & Mortgage Advisor

"I've been looking to get some proper training on FOREX for a while. Most of the courses around seem to offer the earth, cost a fortune and don't exude Trust. I met Siam through an unrelated business and was struck by his honesty and integrity around his experiences of trading. I'm an ex Detective Sergeant and have a really good bullshit detector. I jumped at the chance to learn from him and did his two day course. It delivers in spades. He's very savvy around the subject, has loads of experience to pass on and keeps the training realistic without making stupid promises. If you want FOREX training done properly and realistically, Siam's course is the only place to go bar none. I'm two weeks into my practice account and I'm 1% up. Not bad for a complete newbie after training!"

– Ashley Brown – Director – Kidderminster Builder

"Siam is full of knowledge, a great guy and teacher. The way the course was presented was very professional. It's great value for money, there is no upsell and I have learned lots of new skills and I can't wait to get trading. Siam is also full of knowledge. Great fun!"

– Alex Randisi – Property Investor